PASSWORD
JOURNAL

Speedy Publishing, LLC
40 E Main Street
Newark, Delaware 19711

www.speedypublishing.com

WEB ADDRESS:	
USERNAME:	
PASSWORD:	
SECURITY QUESTION:	
SECURITY ANSWER:	
NOTES:	

WEB ADDRESS:	
USERNAME:	
PASSWORD:	
SECURITY QUESTION:	
SECURITY ANSWER:	
NOTES:	
NOTES:	

WEB ADDRESS:	
USERNAME:	
PASSWORD:	
SECURITY QUESTION:	
SECURITY ANSWER:	
NOTES:	

WEB ADDRESS:	
USERNAME:	
PASSWORD:	
SECURITY QUESTION:	
SECURITY ANSWER:	
NOTES:	
NOTES:	

WEB ADDRESS:	
USERNAME:	
PASSWORD:	
SECURITY QUESTION:	
SECURITY ANSWER:	
NOTES:	

WEB ADDRESS:	
USERNAME:	
PASSWORD:	
SECURITY QUESTION:	
SECURITY ANSWER:	
NOTES:	
NOTES:	

WEB ADDRESS:
USERNAME:
PASSWORD:
SECURITY QUESTION:
SECURITY ANSWER:
NOTES:

WEB ADDRESS:
USERNAME:
PASSWORD:
SECURITY QUESTION:
SECURITY ANSWER:
NOTES:
NOTES:

WEB ADDRESS:
USERNAME:
PASSWORD:
SECURITY QUESTION:
SECURITY ANSWER:
NOTES:

WEB ADDRESS:
USERNAME:
PASSWORD:
SECURITY QUESTION:
SECURITY ANSWER:
NOTES:
NOTES:

WEB ADDRESS:	
USERNAME:	
PASSWORD:	
SECURITY QUESTION:	
SECURITY ANSWER:	
NOTES:	

WEB ADDRESS:	
USERNAME:	
PASSWORD:	
SECURITY QUESTION:	
SECURITY ANSWER:	
NOTES:	
NOTES:	

WEB ADDRESS:	
USERNAME:	
PASSWORD:	
SECURITY QUESTION:	
SECURITY ANSWER:	
NOTES:	

WEB ADDRESS:	
USERNAME:	
PASSWORD:	
SECURITY QUESTION:	
SECURITY ANSWER:	
NOTES:	
NOTES:	

WEB ADDRESS:

USERNAME:

PASSWORD:

SECURITY QUESTION:

SECURITY ANSWER:

NOTES:

WEB ADDRESS:

USERNAME:

PASSWORD:

SECURITY QUESTION:

SECURITY ANSWER:

NOTES:

NOTES:

WEB ADDRESS:

USERNAME:

PASSWORD:

SECURITY QUESTION:

SECURITY ANSWER:

NOTES:

WEB ADDRESS:

USERNAME:

PASSWORD:

SECURITY QUESTION:

SECURITY ANSWER:

NOTES:

NOTES:

WEB ADDRESS:
USERNAME:
PASSWORD:
SECURITY QUESTION:
SECURITY ANSWER:
NOTES:

WEB ADDRESS:
USERNAME:
PASSWORD:
SECURITY QUESTION:
SECURITY ANSWER:
NOTES:
NOTES:

WEB ADDRESS:

USERNAME:

PASSWORD:

SECURITY QUESTION:

SECURITY ANSWER:

NOTES:

WEB ADDRESS:

USERNAME:

PASSWORD:

SECURITY QUESTION:

SECURITY ANSWER:

NOTES:

NOTES:

WEB ADDRESS:
USERNAME:
PASSWORD:
SECURITY QUESTION:
SECURITY ANSWER:
NOTES:

WEB ADDRESS:
USERNAME:
PASSWORD:
SECURITY QUESTION:
SECURITY ANSWER:
NOTES:
NOTES:

WEB ADDRESS:	
USERNAME:	
PASSWORD:	
SECURITY QUESTION:	
SECURITY ANSWER:	
NOTES:	

WEB ADDRESS:	
USERNAME:	
PASSWORD:	
SECURITY QUESTION:	
SECURITY ANSWER:	
NOTES:	
NOTES:	

WEB ADDRESS:
USERNAME:
PASSWORD:
SECURITY QUESTION:
SECURITY ANSWER:
NOTES:

WEB ADDRESS:
USERNAME:
PASSWORD:
SECURITY QUESTION:
SECURITY ANSWER:
NOTES:
NOTES:

WEB ADDRESS:

USERNAME:

PASSWORD:

SECURITY QUESTION:

SECURITY ANSWER:

NOTES:

WEB ADDRESS:

USERNAME:

PASSWORD:

SECURITY QUESTION:

SECURITY ANSWER:

NOTES:

NOTES:

WEB ADDRESS:

USERNAME:

PASSWORD:

SECURITY QUESTION:

SECURITY ANSWER:

NOTES:

WEB ADDRESS:

USERNAME:

PASSWORD:

SECURITY QUESTION:

SECURITY ANSWER:

NOTES:

NOTES:

WEB ADDRESS:

USERNAME:

PASSWORD:

SECURITY QUESTION:

SECURITY ANSWER:

NOTES:

WEB ADDRESS:

USERNAME:

PASSWORD:

SECURITY QUESTION:

SECURITY ANSWER:

NOTES:

NOTES:

WEB ADDRESS:	
USERNAME:	
PASSWORD:	
SECURITY QUESTION:	
SECURITY ANSWER:	
NOTES:	

WEB ADDRESS:	
USERNAME:	
PASSWORD:	
SECURITY QUESTION:	
SECURITY ANSWER:	
NOTES:	
NOTES:	

WEB ADDRESS:

USERNAME:

PASSWORD:

SECURITY QUESTION:

SECURITY ANSWER:

NOTES:

WEB ADDRESS:

USERNAME:

PASSWORD:

SECURITY QUESTION:

SECURITY ANSWER:

NOTES:

NOTES:

WEB ADDRESS:
USERNAME:
PASSWORD:
SECURITY QUESTION:
SECURITY ANSWER:
NOTES:

WEB ADDRESS:
USERNAME:
PASSWORD:
SECURITY QUESTION:
SECURITY ANSWER:
NOTES:
NOTES:

WEB ADDRESS:
USERNAME:
PASSWORD:
SECURITY QUESTION:
SECURITY ANSWER:
NOTES:

WEB ADDRESS:
USERNAME:
PASSWORD:
SECURITY QUESTION:
SECURITY ANSWER:
NOTES:
NOTES:

WEB ADDRESS:
USERNAME:
PASSWORD:
SECURITY QUESTION:
SECURITY ANSWER:
NOTES:

WEB ADDRESS:
USERNAME:
PASSWORD:
SECURITY QUESTION:
SECURITY ANSWER:
NOTES:
NOTES:

WEB ADDRESS:

USERNAME:

PASSWORD:

SECURITY QUESTION:

SECURITY ANSWER:

NOTES:

WEB ADDRESS:

USERNAME:

PASSWORD:

SECURITY QUESTION:

SECURITY ANSWER:

NOTES:

NOTES:

WEB ADDRESS:	
USERNAME:	
PASSWORD:	
SECURITY QUESTION:	
SECURITY ANSWER:	
NOTES:	

WEB ADDRESS:	
USERNAME:	
PASSWORD:	
SECURITY QUESTION:	
SECURITY ANSWER:	
NOTES:	
NOTES:	

WEB ADDRESS:

USERNAME:

PASSWORD:

SECURITY QUESTION:

SECURITY ANSWER:

NOTES:

WEB ADDRESS:

USERNAME:

PASSWORD:

SECURITY QUESTION:

SECURITY ANSWER:

NOTES:

NOTES:

WEB ADDRESS:

USERNAME:

PASSWORD:

SECURITY QUESTION:

SECURITY ANSWER:

NOTES:

WEB ADDRESS:

USERNAME:

PASSWORD:

SECURITY QUESTION:

SECURITY ANSWER:

NOTES:

NOTES:

WEB ADDRESS:

USERNAME:

PASSWORD:

SECURITY QUESTION:

SECURITY ANSWER:

NOTES:

WEB ADDRESS:

USERNAME:

PASSWORD:

SECURITY QUESTION:

SECURITY ANSWER:

NOTES:

NOTES:

WEB ADDRESS:
USERNAME:
PASSWORD:
SECURITY QUESTION:
SECURITY ANSWER:
NOTES:

WEB ADDRESS:
USERNAME:
PASSWORD:
SECURITY QUESTION:
SECURITY ANSWER:
NOTES:
NOTES:

WEB ADDRESS:

USERNAME:

PASSWORD:

SECURITY QUESTION:

SECURITY ANSWER:

NOTES:

WEB ADDRESS:

USERNAME:

PASSWORD:

SECURITY QUESTION:

SECURITY ANSWER:

NOTES:

NOTES:

WEB ADDRESS:	
USERNAME:	
PASSWORD:	
SECURITY QUESTION:	
SECURITY ANSWER:	
NOTES:	

WEB ADDRESS:	
USERNAME:	
PASSWORD:	
SECURITY QUESTION:	
SECURITY ANSWER:	
NOTES:	
NOTES:	

WEB ADDRESS:
USERNAME:
PASSWORD:
SECURITY QUESTION:
SECURITY ANSWER:
NOTES:

WEB ADDRESS:
USERNAME:
PASSWORD:
SECURITY QUESTION:
SECURITY ANSWER:
NOTES:
NOTES:

WEB ADDRESS:

USERNAME:

PASSWORD:

SECURITY QUESTION:

SECURITY ANSWER:

NOTES:

WEB ADDRESS:

USERNAME:

PASSWORD:

SECURITY QUESTION:

SECURITY ANSWER:

NOTES:

NOTES:

WEB ADDRESS:

USERNAME:

PASSWORD:

SECURITY QUESTION:

SECURITY ANSWER:

NOTES:

WEB ADDRESS:

USERNAME:

PASSWORD:

SECURITY QUESTION:

SECURITY ANSWER:

NOTES:

NOTES:

WEB ADDRESS:
USERNAME:
PASSWORD:
SECURITY QUESTION:
SECURITY ANSWER:
NOTES:

WEB ADDRESS:
USERNAME:
PASSWORD:
SECURITY QUESTION:
SECURITY ANSWER:
NOTES:
NOTES:

WEB ADDRESS:	
USERNAME:	
PASSWORD:	
SECURITY QUESTION:	
SECURITY ANSWER:	
NOTES:	

WEB ADDRESS:	
USERNAME:	
PASSWORD:	
SECURITY QUESTION:	
SECURITY ANSWER:	
NOTES:	
NOTES:	

WEB ADDRESS:
USERNAME:
PASSWORD:
SECURITY QUESTION:
SECURITY ANSWER:
NOTES:

WEB ADDRESS:
USERNAME:
PASSWORD:
SECURITY QUESTION:
SECURITY ANSWER:
NOTES:
NOTES:

WEB ADDRESS:

USERNAME:

PASSWORD:

SECURITY QUESTION:

SECURITY ANSWER:

NOTES:

WEB ADDRESS:

USERNAME:

PASSWORD:

SECURITY QUESTION:

SECURITY ANSWER:

NOTES:

NOTES:

WEB ADDRESS:
USERNAME:
PASSWORD:
SECURITY QUESTION:
SECURITY ANSWER:
NOTES:

WEB ADDRESS:
USERNAME:
PASSWORD:
SECURITY QUESTION:
SECURITY ANSWER:
NOTES:
NOTES:

WEB ADDRESS:
USERNAME:
PASSWORD:
SECURITY QUESTION:
SECURITY ANSWER:
NOTES:

WEB ADDRESS:
USERNAME:
PASSWORD:
SECURITY QUESTION:
SECURITY ANSWER:
NOTES:
NOTES:

WEB ADDRESS:	
USERNAME:	
PASSWORD:	
SECURITY QUESTION:	
SECURITY ANSWER:	
NOTES:	

WEB ADDRESS:	
USERNAME:	
PASSWORD:	
SECURITY QUESTION:	
SECURITY ANSWER:	
NOTES:	
NOTES:	

WEB ADDRESS:
USERNAME:
PASSWORD:
SECURITY QUESTION:
SECURITY ANSWER:
NOTES:

WEB ADDRESS:
USERNAME:
PASSWORD:
SECURITY QUESTION:
SECURITY ANSWER:
NOTES:
NOTES:

WEB ADDRESS:
USERNAME:
PASSWORD:
SECURITY QUESTION:
SECURITY ANSWER:
NOTES:

WEB ADDRESS:
USERNAME:
PASSWORD:
SECURITY QUESTION:
SECURITY ANSWER:
NOTES:
NOTES:

WEB ADDRESS:	
USERNAME:	
PASSWORD:	
SECURITY QUESTION:	
SECURITY ANSWER:	
NOTES:	

WEB ADDRESS:	
USERNAME:	
PASSWORD:	
SECURITY QUESTION:	
SECURITY ANSWER:	
NOTES:	
NOTES:	

WEB ADDRESS:
USERNAME:
PASSWORD:
SECURITY QUESTION:
SECURITY ANSWER:
NOTES:

WEB ADDRESS:
USERNAME:
PASSWORD:
SECURITY QUESTION:
SECURITY ANSWER:
NOTES:
NOTES:

WEB ADDRESS:

USERNAME:

PASSWORD:

SECURITY QUESTION:

SECURITY ANSWER:

NOTES:

WEB ADDRESS:

USERNAME:

PASSWORD:

SECURITY QUESTION:

SECURITY ANSWER:

NOTES:

NOTES:

WEB ADDRESS:
USERNAME:
PASSWORD:
SECURITY QUESTION:
SECURITY ANSWER:
NOTES:

WEB ADDRESS:
USERNAME:
PASSWORD:
SECURITY QUESTION:
SECURITY ANSWER:
NOTES:
NOTES:

WEB ADDRESS:

USERNAME:

PASSWORD:

SECURITY QUESTION:

SECURITY ANSWER:

NOTES:

WEB ADDRESS:

USERNAME:

PASSWORD:

SECURITY QUESTION:

SECURITY ANSWER:

NOTES:

NOTES:

WEB ADDRESS:
USERNAME:
PASSWORD:
SECURITY QUESTION:
SECURITY ANSWER:
NOTES:

WEB ADDRESS:
USERNAME:
PASSWORD:
SECURITY QUESTION:
SECURITY ANSWER:
NOTES:
NOTES:

www.ingramcontent.com/pod-product-compliance
Lightning Source LLC
Chambersburg PA
CBHW060444060326
40690CB00019B/4330